Vikings

Kath Davies

Illustrations by
Roger Payne

A ZOË BOOK

A *ZOË BOOK*

©1995 Zoë Books Limited

Devised and produced by
Zoë Books Limited
15 Worthy Lane
Winchester
Hampshire SO23 7AB
England

Illustrative material used in this book first appeared in *History Detective: Over 900 Years Ago With The Vikings*, published by Zoë Books Limited.

First published in Great Britain in 1995 by
Zoë Books Limited
15 Worthy Lane
Winchester
Hampshire SO23 7AB

A record of the CIP data is available from the British Library.

ISBN 1 874488 40 1

Printed in Italy by Grafedit SpA
Edited by Imogen Dawson
Design: Julian Holland
Production: Grahame Griffiths

Photographic acknowledgements

The publishers wish to acknowledge, with thanks, the following photographic sources:

7 Werner Forman Archive/Viking Ship Museum, Bygody; 11 Statens Historiska Museum, Stockholm; 14 Werner Forman Archive/Statens Historiska Museum, Stockholm; 19 Robert Harding Picture Library; 23, 27 Ancient Art and Architecture Collection.

CONTENTS

Ships and Shipbuilding

The Vikings lived more than 900 years ago. They lived in the countries which are now called Norway, Sweden and Denmark.

It was difficult for people to travel on land in these countries, because there were thick forests and high mountains. Travelling by water was much easier, and most Vikings lived near the sea. They were very good shipbuilders.

The Vikings were also farmers, who grew their own food. In winter and in early spring, there was not much work to do on the farms. The Vikings often built new ships at this time of the year. Sometimes they worked in a special boat shed, but usually they worked in the open air.

The Vikings used the trunk of a large oak tree to make the bottom, or **keel**, of the ship. They nailed on planks for the sides. Wooden pieces called **ribs** were nailed across the planks to keep them in shape. The ships were strong. They could sail on rivers and lakes, as well as on the sea.

On board ship

The Vikings sailed west and north, to Iceland, Greenland and to North America. In the east, they travelled along the rivers of Russia. Some Vikings reached the cities of Istanbul and Baghdad, across the Black Sea and the Caspian Sea. The Vikings sailed further than any other Europeans of their time.

▼ The axe was used to chop down trees, and to split the trunks into planks.

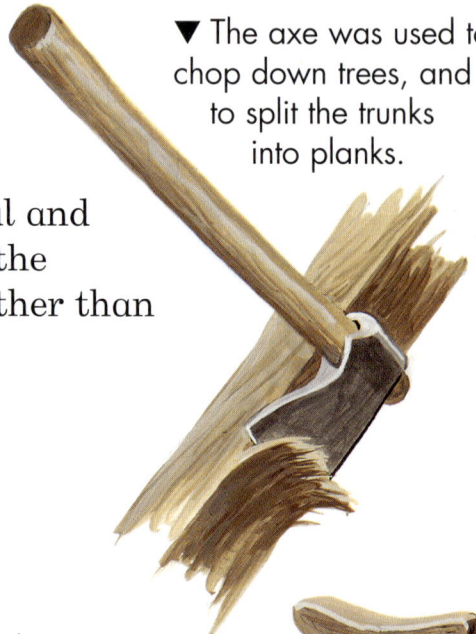

▼ The adze made curved shapes in pieces of wood.

▶ The auger made holes in the wood. Then wooden pegs or iron nails were knocked in.

▼ These moulding irons cut grooves in the wood, to decorate it.

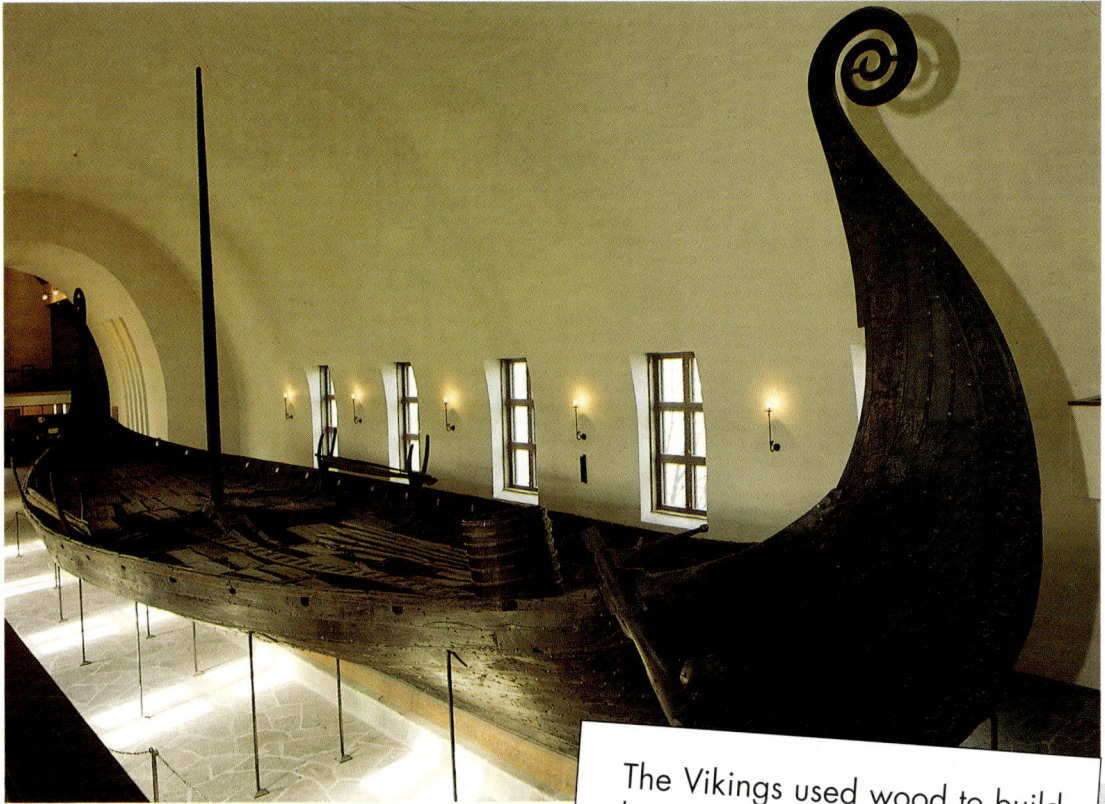

▲ The Oseberg ship

A Viking ship had a square woollen sail. There were oars for rowing, and a large paddle, or **rudder**, to steer the ship. The sailors used sleeping-bags made from animal skins.

Many Vikings believed that when they died, they would travel in a ship to another life.

The Oseberg ship

People who study the things from the past are called **archaeologists**. About

The Vikings used wood to build houses and ships. They often used wooden pegs instead of nails.

Look at the picture on pages 4 and 5. How many different ways are the Vikings using wood?

HISTORY STARTERS

90 years ago, archaeologists found a Viking ship in Norway. The ship was buried at Oseberg, about 1100 years ago. It held everything that a **royal** woman would need on her journey to the next life.

Raiders

About 1150 years ago, the Viking population was growing. The land could not provide enough food for everyone. Some Vikings tried to make a living another way. They began to make attacks, or **raids**, on other people's homes and goods.

The first raid we know about happened in AD 793. The Vikings attacked a **monastery** at Lindisfarne (Holy Island) off the coast of north east England. They stole treasure from the church and killed some of the **monks**. The Vikings made more raids.

They sailed to France, to Germany and the Netherlands. At first the Vikings attacked only monasteries, which were not well guarded. Then the Vikings grew more daring. They attacked towns and cities too.

In AD 834 they raided Dorestad in the Netherlands. In 835 the Vikings attacked towns around the coast of Britain. After the raids, they sailed home with the stolen goods.

In 845, the Vikings found another way to make money. They surrounded Paris, in France, and they did not leave until the French king paid 3000 kilograms of silver. They began to do this in other places as well.

The money which was paid to the Vikings to make them go away became known as **Danegeld**. During the next 200 years, the kings of England paid the Danes huge amounts of this money.

9

Weapons and armour

The raiders used swords and battle-axes. They also had spears and large knives. The raiders protected their bodies with wooden shields. Some fighters wore shirts called birnies. These shirts were made from small pieces of metal linked together, or **chain-mail**. Birnies cost a lot of silver. On their heads, the Vikings wore helmets made of iron or leather.

▲ A Viking battle-axe could chop through shields and helmets.

▶ Spears were thrown in battle. They were also used to stab enemies.

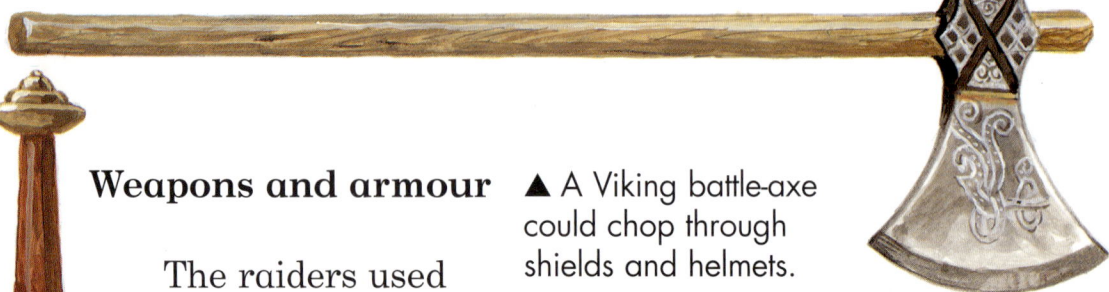

◀ Swords were made from rods of iron. They had steel edges. Sometimes the handle, or hilt, was decorated in silver or gold. Swords had names, such as 'Leg-biter'.

▶ Shields were made from wood and iron.

▶ This stone is at Lingsberg in Sweden. The Viking writing on the stone says that it is in memory of a Viking called Ulvrik. The writing says that he was given two payments of Danegeld in England.

For hundreds of years, people did not know much about the Viking people. The monks wrote about the Viking raids. They did not write about how the Vikings lived. Today, archaeologists have found other **evidence** which shows that the Vikings were not all fierce fighters.

What do you think the Vikings did with the things they stole? What goods did they need to buy with the Danegeld? You will find some of these goods in the pictures on pages 6 and 10.

HISTORY STARTERS

Traders

Vikings from Sweden travelled to the East. They crossed the Baltic Sea to Russia, where they traded with the people who lived there. The Vikings then sailed along rivers such as the Volga and the Dnieper. By about AD 860, they had reached the city of Istanbul. They called this famous trading centre Miklagard.

The traders brought furs, silver, wax or honey, to buy or exchange for gold, wine, **spices** and jewels. They also bought silks which came from China.

When they had bought all the goods they could afford, the Viking traders returned to Sweden. They sold some of their goods on the way back, in markets at towns such as Kiev and Novgorod. Most of the goods were taken to the market at Birka, in Sweden.

People came to Birka market from all over the Viking world. The traders sold their goods from the East, and bought more goods. Then they set out again for the East.

Silver and glass

Archaeologists have dug out, or **excavated**, some of the Viking towns, such as Hedeby in Denmark, Dublin in Ireland and York in England.

They have found out where the Vikings traded by studying the things that they excavated. For example, in York, which the Vikings called Jorvik, they found silk from China and coins from Russia.

The Vikings were buried with objects which were made of glass, pottery and metal. Archaeologists know that these objects, or **artefacts**, came from different places.

▲ Glass jars like these came from Birka. They were probably made in eastern Europe.

▼ This horn was found in the grave of a Viking man. The horn was full of silver coins from many countries.

Many stories were told about the Vikings. These stories, or **sagas**, were first told in Viking times. They were written down later, about 700 years ago.

Most of the sagas are about the Vikings who sailed to Iceland. There were hardly any trees for shipbuilding in Iceland. The Vikings in Iceland traded smoked and dried fish for wood from Britain and Norway.

People came to market to buy and sell goods, and to hear all the news from the travellers. Some of these goods have been found by archaeologists.

How many different goods can you see in the picture on pages 12 and 13?

HISTORY STARTERS

▲ These scales fold up into the carrying case. Traders took scales with them to markets.

◀ Viking traders weighed coins. They did not give any change. They sometimes cut up the coins to make the right weight of silver. They used coins from any country. Silver jewellery was also used as money. It was called hack-silver.

Settlers

The Viking lands were becoming very crowded. There was not enough farmland to grow crops to feed all the people. About 1100 years ago, some people decided to find other places where they could live.

Not many people lived in the Orkney and Shetland Islands, off the north coast of Scotland. Some of the Vikings settled there. They took their families, farm animals, tools and weapons with them. Other Vikings settled along the coast of Scotland, on the Western Isles and on the Isle of Man. They set up a trading centre at Dublin in Ireland.

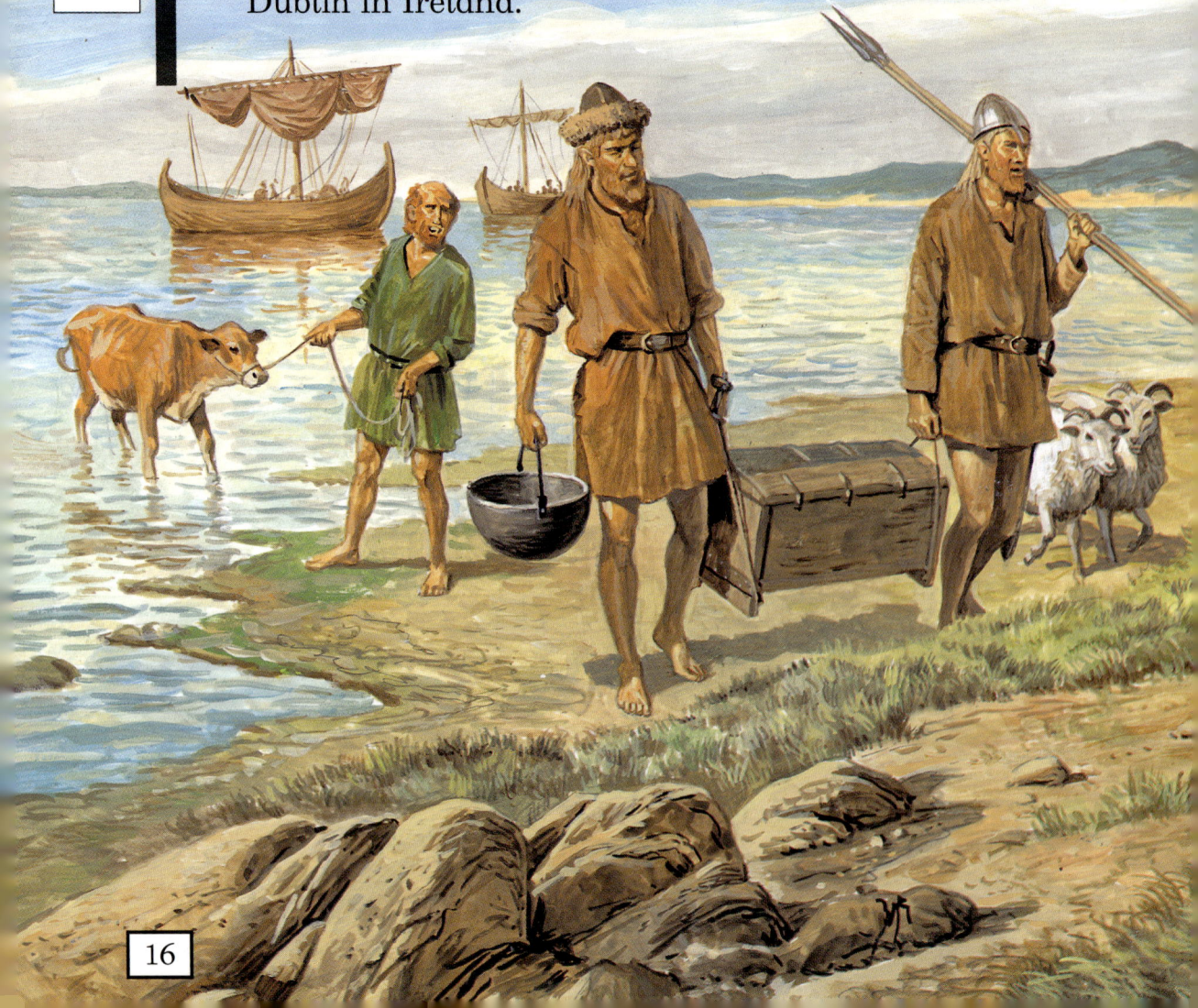

Many Danish Vikings settled in eastern England about 1150 years ago. The area became known as the **Danelaw**.

Vikings from Norway settled in Iceland. In AD 982, a Viking called Eirik the Red was sent away from Iceland. He was an **outlaw**. Eirik went to live in Greenland, where other Vikings soon joined him.

In about AD 1000, Eirik's son, Leif, was the first Viking to land in North America. Leif landed at a place he called Markland. It may have been in Newfoundland. He travelled south to **Vinland**. The Vikings spent about two years in North America.

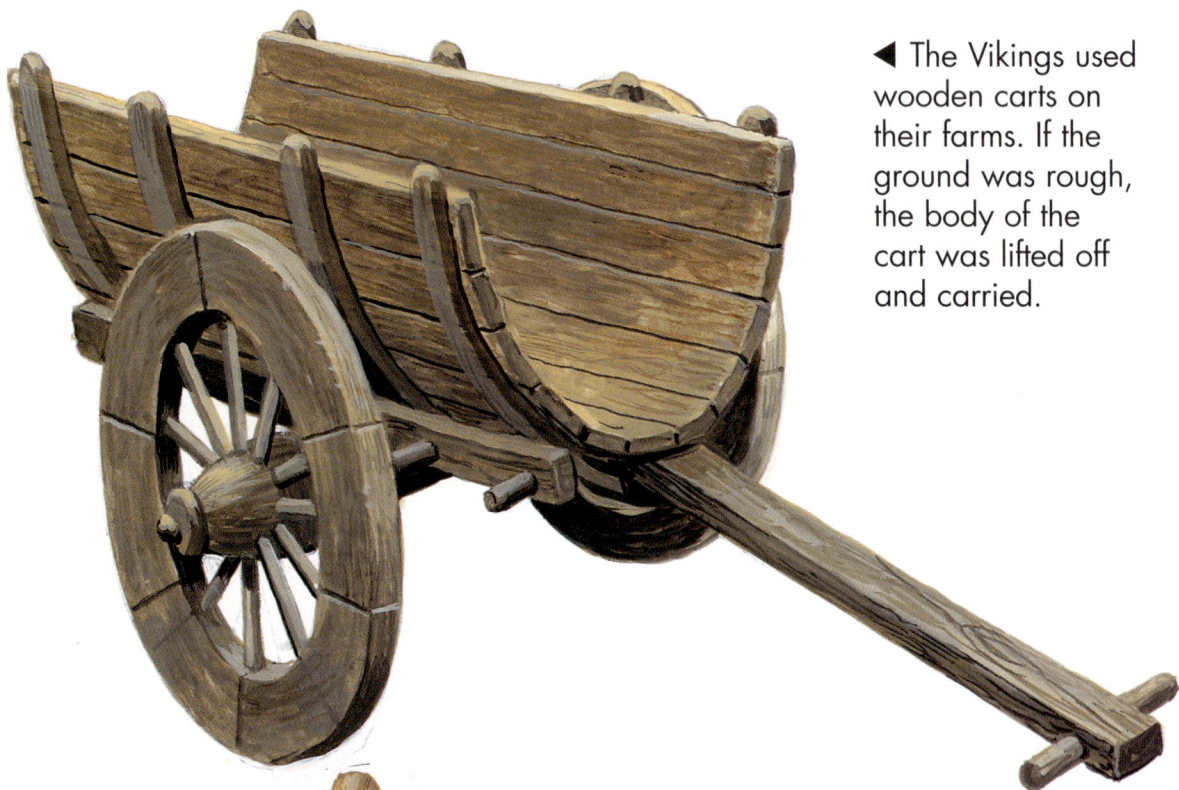

◀ The Vikings used wooden carts on their farms. If the ground was rough, the body of the cart was lifted off and carried.

Farming new lands

Some of the Vikings settled in towns. They were craft workers and traders. Most of the settlers were farmers.

The Vikings used wood, stone or blocks of **turf** for building. They built a **longhouse** for the family, and barns for the animals. They also built a place in which to make and to mend iron tools. This was called a **smithy**.

The Vikings grew cabbages and onions near their houses. They put up fences and made fields, to grow crops such as

▲ Farmers often found pieces of **iron ore** in bogs. They used it to make tools like these.

▲ A Viking farmhouse at Stong in Iceland may have looked like this.

oats and barley. Most animals were killed in the autumn, because there was not enough food for them in the winter.

The Vikings who settled in England mixed with the English people. Words such as 'bread', 'egg' and 'sky' are Viking words.

The Vikings who went to Iceland kept their own beliefs and customs. They set up local meetings, called **Things**. The Things made laws which all the people agreed to obey. In AD 1000 the Vikings in Iceland agreed at their Thing to become **Christians**.

Archaeologists have found evidence about how the Vikings built their farms. The Viking farmhouse at Stong has been rebuilt, or **reconstructed**, using this evidence.

Look at the pictures on pages 16, 17 and 18. What other things have archaeologists found out about Viking settlers?

HISTORY STARTERS

The Vikings at Home

The first Viking houses had only one room. The family ate and slept in it. Children, parents and grandparents all lived together. The women worked at home during the day and took care of the children. Children helped with the work. They did not go to school.

The room had an open fire which burned in a long hearth in the middle of the floor. There was no chimney. The smoke from the fire went out through a hole in the roof, but the room was often full of smoke. It was dark because there were no windows. The floor was made of earth.

There was not much furniture. A bench along the walls was used for seats in the daytime. At night, people slept on the bench.

Clothes and blankets were hung on hooks on the walls. There were no cupboards.

Viking women

Viking women chose their own husbands. They also had the right to **divorce** their husbands. As well as looking after the home and the children, they also worked on the farm. They took charge when the men were away.

Women made all the clothes for the family. The men and the boys wore woollen tunics and trousers. Women and girls wore a woollen tunic over a long linen dress. In cold weather, the women also wore woollen shawls.

▲ Viking women wove cloth on looms like this one. Women and children spun the wool into yarn. They coloured it with dyes made from plants.

▼ Food was stored in wooden barrels and boxes. Wood was also used for spoons and plates. A wooden cheese drainer is next to the axe.

It took a long time to prepare and to cook food. The women ground barley and oats with stones called **querns**. They made bread and porridge. The bread was baked on a flat stone slab which was placed over the fire.

Cooking pans were made of metal. Meat was stewed in a pot. Vegetables such as onions or peas were added to it.

The women also made butter, cheese and beer.

When work was over, people told stories or played board games. Musical instruments and games have been found.

Look at the pictures on this page and on pages 20 and 21. Write about a day in a Viking home.

HISTORY STARTERS

▼ The fire gave light and heat. It was the centre of family life. This model is at York (Jorvik).

Viking Crafts

People made almost everything they needed. However, some things, such as jewellery or weapons, were made by craft workers. They usually lived in towns, where there were plenty of people to buy their goods.

Archaeologists have found that in towns such as Hedeby and York, the craft workers had workshops behind their homes. They sold their goods from stalls which they set up on the street in front of their houses.

There were shoemakers, woodworkers, bone-carvers and blacksmiths, as well as jewellers. The blacksmiths worked on the edge of town, so that there was less danger from their fires.

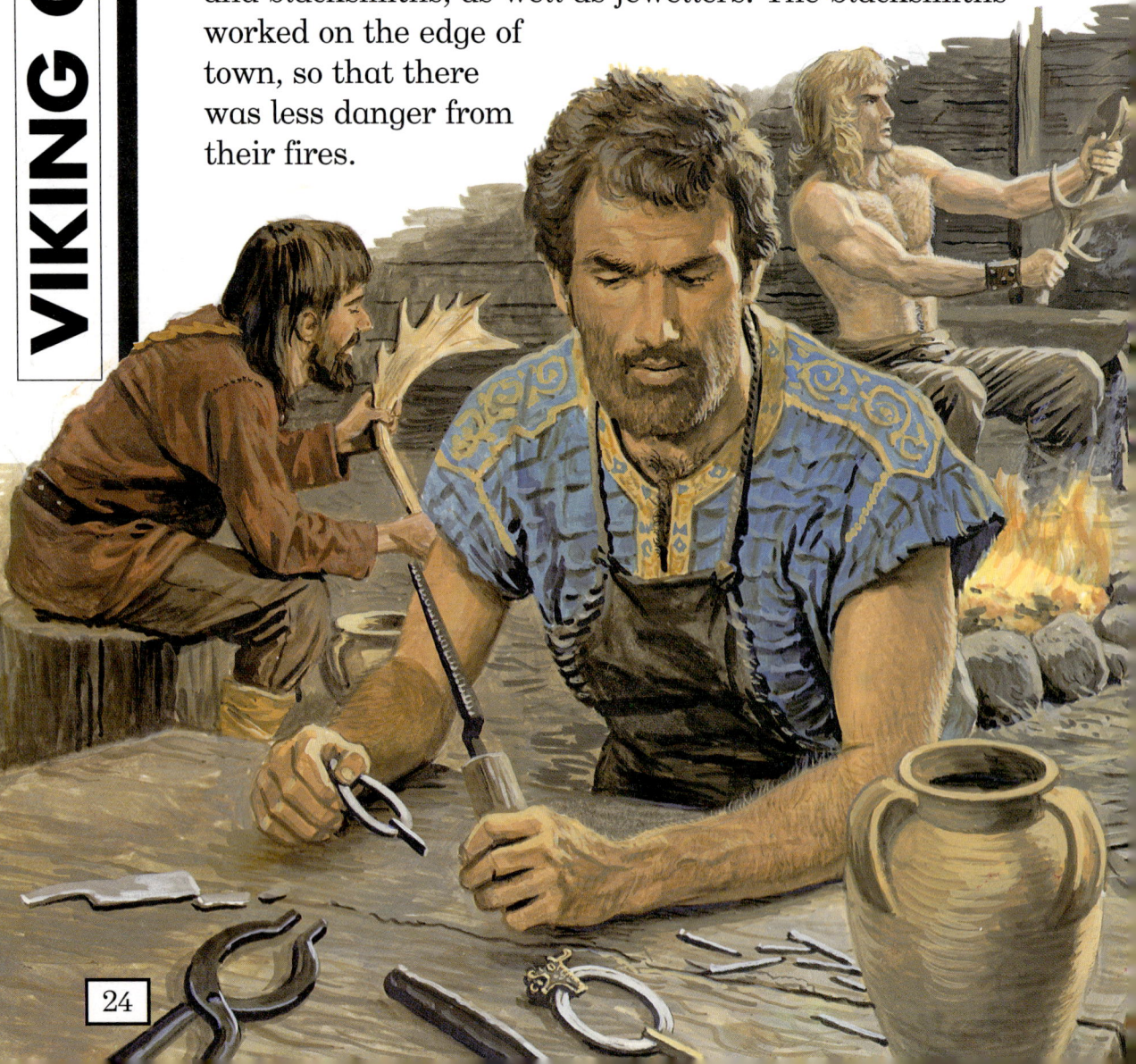

The craft workers used natural materials such as wood, bones and deer antlers.

Craftworkers sold goods to traders, who took them to other towns or to farms to sell.

The Viking alphabet had 16 letters, or **runes**. Craftworkers carved runes on many objects. They show people that these objects were made by Vikings.

Bones and jewellery

The bones came from animals which had been killed for food and for skins. The antlers were picked up in the woods. Every year, the deer drop, or shed, their antlers.

The foot bones of cattle and horses were made into ice-skates. Other bones were used for making combs, needles and buckles.

▼ Buckles were made from bones or antlers. They were carved, or coloured with dyes.

▲ People said the Vikings were proud of the way they looked. Combs like these were found in all the places where the Vikings settled.

All Vikings liked to wear jewellery. It showed how rich they were, but jewellery was also useful.

Both women and men used brooches to hold their clothes together. They hung keys,

▶ This jewellery was found in the grave of a Viking woman in Birka. Beads were made from silver or glass. The Vikings bought pieces of glass from Italy and Germany, to make the beads.

needle-cases and combs on a brooch and chain. Their clothes did not have pockets. Rich people had silver and gold brooches. Poor people wore brooches made from cheaper metals, such as lead.

Before they became Christians, the Vikings worshipped their own gods. Thor was a favourite god. He carried a hammer which he called 'Mjollni'. Many Vikings wore Mjollni charms around their necks.

Odin or Wodin, the god of war, was the most important Viking god. Thor was the god of thunder. Freya was the goddess of love. Which days of the week are named after these Viking gods and goddesses?

HISTORY STARTERS

Time Line

AD

700–800 Many people begin to look for new lands where they could farm, or for other ways of making a living.

793 Viking raiders attack the monastery at Lindisfarne (Holy Island), off the north east coast of England.

800 Vikings settle in the Orkney and Shetland Islands, to the north of Scotland.

835 Start of 15 years of Viking raids on Britain.

844 Viking raiders reach Spain. They are defeated at the town of Cordoba, by the Moorish people who live there.

845 Vikings besiege Paris.

850 Vikings spend the winter in England. Vikings from Sweden begin to visit Russia.

860 Vikings from Norway reach Iceland. Swedish Vikings reach Instanbul.

867 A Viking army captures York.

878 King Alfred the Great defeats the Vikings. He allows them to settle in eastern England. The area is known as the Danelaw.

901	Edward, King of part of England called Wessex, starts to recapture the Danelaw.
911	Vikings are allowed to settle in France.
954	The last Viking King of York, Eirik Bloodaxe, is killed at the battle of Stainmore.
980	Christianity spreads through Viking lands.
985	Vikings from Iceland settle in Greenland.
991	More Viking attacks on Britain.
1000	Leif Eiriksson sails to Vinland.
1016	The Danish Viking king, Svein Forkbeard, becomes king of England and Denmark. His son Canute, and his grandson, Harthacanute, rule England.
1042	Edward the Confessor is chosen as king in England.
1066	William of Normandy conquers England. Viking raids come to an end.

Glossary

GLOSSARY

AD: stands for Anno Domini which means 'in the year of our Lord'. The years in the Christian calendar are counted from the year in which they believe Christ was born. AD is used to show that the year was after the birth of Christ. BC stands for Before Christ. It is used to show that the year was before the birth of Christ.

archaeologist: someone who studies objects and buildings from the past.

artefacts: objects which have been made by people.

chain-mail: tiny links of metal. A shirt made of this protected the wearer from injury in battle.

Christian: someone who follows the religion which was started by Jesus Christ.

Danegeld: money that rulers paid to the Vikings to stop them from attacking their lands.

Danelaw: the part of England where Vikings from Denmark lived. It included the towns of Derby, Lincoln, Leicester, Nottingham and Stamford.

divorce: the end by law of a marriage between a husband and wife.

evidence: proof that something happened.

excavate: to dig up buried objects in a careful way, in order to find out more about the past.

iron ore: rock which contains the metal, iron.

keel: the lowest part of a boat which runs along the whole length of the boat. The keel supports the whole framework of the boat.

longhouse: a Viking farmhouse. It was long and narrow in shape.

monastery: the buildings where monks live (see **monk**).

monk: a man who has decided to follow a religious way of life. He usually lives with other men in a monastery. Women who live in this way are called **nuns**. They live in **convents**.

outlaw: someone who broke the law. Outlaws were usually sent out of the country. If they did not leave, it was not a crime to kill them.

quern: two hard stones which were used to grind grain. The grain was put between them. The stones were turned round and round by hand, until the grain became fine flour.

raid: a sudden attack on a place. The raiders stole anything they could find.

reconstruct: to rebuild something so that it looks the same as it did when it was first built.

rib: a curved part of the side of a boat which runs from the keel at the bottom of the boat to the deck at the top.

royal: to do with a king or queen.

rudder: a flat piece of wood or metal at the back of a boat which is used to control the direction the boat takes.

runes: the letters of the Viking alphabet. They were stick-like in shape, so they were easy to carve on wood, stone or metal.

sagas: stories of Viking adventures. At first they were learned by heart. Some sagas were written down about 700 years ago.

smithy: the place where a blacksmith works. It has a very hot fire, or forge, on which iron is heated to make or mend tools and other things made of iron.

spices: seeds, leaves or roots, used in cooking to add flavour to food.

Thing: a meeting where Vikings made laws and settled arguments between local people.

turf: a piece of grass and earth.

Vinland: the name which Leif Eiriksson gave to part of North America. No one knows for certain where it was. The area was probably to the south of Newfoundland.

Index